FundaMENUS cover & layout design, logo,
photography, artwork & recipes by Jody McFerren
Buffet photograph on page 100 by Renny Hart

*Funda*MENUS

An *Upscale*
Approach
to **Affordable**
Entertaining

*To Alan,
Good luck
& Happy
Cooking*

Jody Robert McFerren

$\mathcal{F}$unda**MENUS**

$\mathcal{A}$cknowledgments

My life has always guided me in a very artistic direction. It has shaped me into the strong, gay man that I am today. My artistic and culinary creativity has given me the opportunity to publish my very first cookbook. My cookbook is about more than just food, however. It is also about sharing unforgettable moments with very special people. There are so many people that have helped and inspired me while I was writing this book and I would like to thank each and every one of them. I am humbled and extremely honored to dedicate this book to my friends and family. Thank you all so very much for being a part of my culinary history!

First and foremost, I would like to thank my mom and dad. I am very proud to have you both as my parents.

To my Father - Thank you for being a hard worker. Your work ethic is unparalleled and I learned that from you. Also, thank you for accepting me for who I am. I may not have always been the son that you imagined having, but I am glad that you always say otherwise.

To my Mother - Thank you for always being my inspiration. I learned how to cook because of you and you have always allowed me to be the creative individual that I was meant to be. I love you dearly.

To my Sisters, Lacy, Shawn & Bobbi - Thank you for being loving siblings. I value each of our friendships and thank you all for lifting me up when I need it. Much love to all three of you.

To my Brother-in-Law, Brian - Thank you for being a big brother.

To Pap & Grandma - Thank you for being the best grandparents in the world. I am blessed to have you in my life.

To my Nieces, Skye, Rayna, Haley & Emma - Your uncle is so lucky to have the best nieces. Keep shining bright.

To Pat Heefner & Karen Scott - The two of you were my mentors and friends while I was in high school and both of you always told me that I was something special. Thank you so much for making me believe that! The two of you are constantly in my thoughts.

To the "Pooses" - Rosalind, Heather & Amy - I am so glad that we are so close, even after all these years. True friends are hard to come by and when I get down, all I have to do is call upon one of my Pooses to lift me back up again. Love you gals!

To my Friends - Christa (Xta), Janell & Frank, Michael Fletcher, Renny & Andy, George & Kathleen, Kim, Salvador, Amy & Kevin, Beth & John, Little Jen & Isaac, Ann S., Dan & Roy, my friends from AIP, Michael Diebert, Teresa Conklin, Dennis & Ed, Scott & Azi, Don & Teresa, Chris, Paul & Jason, Eva, Rebecca, Dave Radlmann, Hunter & Jen, all of my "special" friends from Burning Man, Trish, Whitney Morris, Chuck Milne, Rock-n-Roll Heather, Chef Cry, Meg & Timo, my friends from WASHS, Julie, Neen & Joe, Favorite & Ben, Angel & Ryan, Jason & Andy, Heather & Jon, Heath, Brian & Toyo, Frank Golley, Bryan & Michelle, Lamirand, the entire Drunken Phoenix Dart Team and all the fine folks that I met along the way - Special friends are measured by how much they support you through the good times and stick by your side through the bad times. Having you all in my life is why life is so darn great. Cheers!

To Fernando Hildebrand - You are my best friend. You make me a better man. I value our friendship so much. I am honored to be your Granny McFerren. Thank you for being a true friend. Much love.

To my Publicist, Jennifer Perry - When it comes to boosting my ego, you take the cake. I am so glad you chose me to be your client. More importantly, thank you for your friendship. Love ya honey.

To my Inspirations - Betty White, Dolly Parton, Janet Jackson, Suzanne Vega, George Michael, The B-52's, Donna Summer, Doris Day, Mariah Carey, Sade, Stevie Nicks, Deee-Lite, Judy Garland, Cher, Kathy Griffin, Xtina Aguilera, Beyonce, Cathy Dennis, Madonna, Pink, Whitney Houston, Adam Ant, Britney Spears, Barbara Mandrell, Rock Hudson, Andy Cohen & Elvis Presley - All of you have been my true inspirations throughout my entire life. At least one of you have been playing somewhere in the background during my creative moments. Many thanks!

*In loving memory of my dear friend, **Ruth Golley.***
You will always be remembered. Thank you for all of our
wonderful conversations while sharing great food.

*Funda*MENUS

Contents

*Funda*MENUS

Chapter 1

An Introduction to Affordable Entertaining

t's true. The thought of hosting a dinner party for six or more people can seem like an overwhelming and intimidating ordeal. Throw in a lagging economy and the fact that food costs have risen while most job salaries have not, getting a good group of friends together for an evening of upscale, socialization may seem like a thing of the past. But, what most people don't realize is, that preparing an upscale, four-course dinner for 10 to 12 people can be achieved with very little effort, minimal stress and a lot less money than one might expect. It just requires a bit more creativity and outside-of-the-box thinking.

I am proof of this mentality. In the past, I have had the misfortune of being unemployed for over a year and my finances were not what they used to be. However, over the course of that year, I hosted three dinner parties that did not affect my tight, financial budget. The smallest dinner party I threw was for 12 people and the largest was a Christmas party buffet that fed 50 guests. The buffet had 18 different recipes ranging from savory appetizers to sinfully-sweet desserts. My price tag for that

Christmas dinner buffet, one might ask? Well, it was a very affordable $150! And that was including the alcohol! That dollar amount may seem "too good to be true" for most people to believe, but the truth is, all dinner parties have the same thing in common... A **FundaMENU**.

FundaMENUS

A **FundaMENU** simply means sharing ingredients between two or more dinner courses. A more cost-effective approach to entertaining can be achieved by doubling, tripling or even quadrupling-up on ingredients from one course and incorporating the same ingredients into another. For example, for one of my upscale, sit-down dinner parties, my salad course was an avocado salad with cilantro & lime vinaigrette. The avocado, cilantro and lime also made appearances in my soup course which was an avocado & lime chili, my main course, a delicious lime & cilantro tuna ceviche with a fried avocado, and even in my dessert course, which was a lime, avocado cheesecake garnished with a sprig of cilantro. By incorporating three ingredients on my dinner menu, I saved myself a lot of money and my guests were impressed by the way the flavors of every dish grew in intensity from one course to the next.

I devised my **FundaMENU** approach to upscale dining many years ago, mainly out of necessity. I had co-owned a catering company and restaurant for eight years and because of the rising food costs, I had to think of a more profitable way that would create flavorful, upscale menus for my clients without having to raise my catering prices. That way, my clients were happy and I was able to make a decent profit for my hard work.

Know Where to Shop

Besides devising a smart menu for a dinner party, another important issue when hosting a dinner event is knowing where to shop for ingredients and party accessories. Because I live in a city, I realize that I have a better opportunity for finding a bargain when it comes to ingredients. However,

I was born and raised in a small town and I do know that getting a good deal on food is also tangible for people that live in sparsely-populated areas. For me, to get the best bang for my buck, I shop at three or four different places. After preparing my **FundaMENU**, I separate my list of items into three categories. My categories are labeled as follows: **Grocery Store**, **Farmer's Market**, **Dollar Store/Other**.

The first category is the **Grocery Store**. In my case, I shop at **Kroger**. I live less than a mile from my closest **Kroger Shopping Center**, which is extremely time and cost effective. I buy all my red meats, pork, chicken, dairy products, most breads, most condiments, some party favors and wine and beer at this particular supermarket. Grocery stores have the best deals on meats, especially chicken and pork.

The second category of knowing where to shop is at the **Farmer's Market**. I happen to live only three blocks away from a large, farmer's market, which makes me the luckiest man on earth. I buy all of my vegetables, most grains, herbs and spices, fish and seafood at the Farmer's Market. The prices on these items are normally 30-50% lower than shopping for the same ingredients at a grocery store. For example, limes at a grocery store are usually three limes for one dollar. At the farmer's market, limes are usually 10 cents per lime. That is a great deal in any world!

The final category that I place the remaining items on my shopping list is the **Dollar Store/Other**. Dollar stores are everywhere these days. In fact, my small town where I grew up located in Waynesboro, Pennsylvania, has had one for years. This is the place where I buy napkins, olives, cake mixes, some spices, zip-lock bags, dinner party favors, ect. Time and time again, I have saved one to four dollars on just one item, making the dollar store a "must shop" location for every dinner party engagement.

If I can't find what I want at the dollar store then the "**Other**" store category comes into play. For me these stores include **Walmart** and the closest Asian market. But, to be completely honest, it is very rare that I even need to use these options.

Preparation & Timing

Any host will tell you that preparation and timing are the keys to creating a successful dinner party. That is why I choose a food menu that can be made in advance for at least two or three of my dinner courses that I plan to serve on the evening of my party. If I am serving cocktails instead of wine, I prepare those recipes a day or two ahead of time as well.

The main course is always the course that I choose to cook fresh while the guests are arriving and enjoying cocktails. That way they get the impression that I slaved all day in the kitchen just to make them happy. Having only one item to prepare on the day of the dinner party is essential. A good host is just that... Not a person trapped in a kitchen the whole evening and not being able to enjoy social time with dinner guests.

When it comes to the salad course, I prep all of the salad ingredients in advance and store them in separate containers until just before the guests arrive. If a salad recipe contains fruits or vegetables that tend to rust, I simply add lime juice to them before placing them into their storage bags or containers.

The soup course is always made ahead of time. Because soups are freezer-friendly, I usually prepare the soup course a week or two in advance, placing it into the freezer until I am ready to thaw it out the day before. A few hours before guests arrive, I place the thawed soup into a crock pot or heat it on the stove top until it is ready to serve.

Dessert is my favorite course of the evening. And for me, it is the easiest to prepare. Just make sure to make it in advance. Most desserts are so inexpensive to make and give the appearance that a lot of time and effort was spent in the kitchen. Homemade cakes, pies, cookies, cobblers and bread puddings are the least time-consuming sweets and are usually the most popular with dinner guests. Make sure to present them well by placing them onto some unique platters or cake stands.

If you are attempting to add an an appetizer course to one of the four-course **FundaMENU** scenarios, you must first choose an appetizer that you feel comfortable with making. All of my recipes are relatively easy to prepare, but some appetizers are easier to plate that others. The appetizers that I have provided in this book can all be prepped in advance. When serving the appetizer of choice at a dinner party, make sure to pull all the serving plates needed for the evening and place them in an accessible location for quick and easy plating. Also make sure to precut any garnishes such as herbs and prepare any sauces that may be used for the dishes that you may be serving that evening.

FundaMENUS are specifically designed food scenarios that will give every new party entertainer the confidence to host a party like a pro or allow the experienced host the much needed time to socialize with the people that they love the most. After all, isn't that what entertaining for friends and family is all about anyway?

Now that you have a knowledge of entertaining basics, it is time to host a dinner party. Let the entertaining begin!

For Recipe Photography
& Entertaining Tips. Log onto...

FundaMENUS.COM

*Funda*MENUS

Chapters 2-7

Four-Course Dinner Parties

he following chapters of **FundaMENUS** focuses on the four-course dinner party. I have included seven, four-course dinner party menus that even a person who is new to hosting and preparing large-party, sit-down dinners, can handle with ease and confidence. My recipes are simple, easy to prepare and above all, can work on any budget. Believe me, my money may not go as far as it used to, but sharing moments with loved ones over great food is a part of good living... It just needs to be "spent" wisely, in both senses of the word.

Within this book, I have also included seven, economically-friendly and delicious appetizers that can be substituted for a dinner course or can be added to each **FundaMENU**. I do recommend, however, that only the more skilled dinner party entertainers attempt adding an appetizer to the **FundaMENUS**. Too much, too soon is never a good thing.

*Funda*MENU **1**

Asian Inspiration

Salad Course
Cucumber & Dill Salad

☾

Soup Course
Thai Peanut Soup

☾

Main Course
Spicy Cajun Curry Chicken with Basmati Dill Rice

☾

Dessert Course
Coconut Custard Cake

Cucumber & Dill Salad

4	large seedless cucumbers, sliced
3	T fresh dill, chopped
1/2	large, yellow onion, sliced
2	cups white wine vinegar
1	T sugar
1	t white pepper
1/2	t sea salt

Slice onions and cucumbers and place in mixing bowl. Stir in remaining ingredients. Cover and place in refrigerator overnight. Place salad into 12 small bowls. Garnish with fresh dill. Serves 12.

Thai Peanut Soup

1	cup onion, chopped
1	cup celery, chopped
1	cup red bell pepper, chopped
2	T butter
3	T flour
1	t red pepper
1/4	t salt
6	cups chicken stock
1	16 oz. can coconut milk
1	16 oz. can cream of coconut
2	T lemon grass (out of tube)
1	cup creamy peanut butter
4	cups cooked chicken, shredded
2	T Worcestershire sauce
3	T soy sauce
2	bunches fresh cilantro, chopped

In large pot, saute the first four ingredients over medium heat. Incorporate flour until mixture thickens. Gradually add remaining ingredients to pot, ending with the peanut butter, stirring between each addition. In frying pan over medium heat, combine cooked chicken, Worcestershire sauce, soy sauce and cilantro. Allow ingredients to heat and place into pot with remaining ingredients. Simmer for 10 minutes. Remove from heat and serve. Makes 12 large servings.

Spicy Cajun Curry Chicken

6	boneless chicken breasts
2	sticks butter
2	green bell peppers, sliced into thin strips
1	small yellow onion, diced
3	T Caribbean jerk seasoning
2	t seasoned salt
2	T curry powder
2	medium cans crushed tomatoes
2	cups water

Preheat oven to 350 degrees F. Place chicken breasts onto a greased baking sheet and bake for 35 minutes. Take out of oven to cool. Tear chicken into pieces and set aside. In large saucepan, melt butter, bell peppers and onion. Add jerk seasoning, seasoned salt, curry powder, crushed tomatoes and water. Add chicken pieces to the mixture and simmer on medium heat for 30 minutes, stirring every five minutes until chicken melds into mixture. Serve on top of any rice. Makes 12 servings.

Basmati Dill Rice

3	cups chicken broth
3	T butter
1/2	t salt
2	cups Basmati rice
1	T lemon zest
2	T fresh dill, chopped
1/2	t nutmeg

Place rice in large bowl and cover with cold water. Allow rice to set for 10 minutes, stirring halfway through. Drain water from rice. Repeat the process two more times. Place broth, butter, and salt in a large saucepan. Bring to a boil over high heat. Stir in rice and reduce heat to low. Cover rice and simmer for 25 minutes or until broth mixture is absorbed and rice is tender. Remove from heat and using a fork, toss with lemon zest, nutmeg and dill. Serves 12.

Coconut Custard Cake

1/2	box (18.5 oz.) white cake mix
1/2	cup coconut cream
4	eggs
1	cup sugar
1	t almond extract
1	t vanilla extract
1	cup milk
1 1/4	cup sweetened coconut, flaked
1	cup (2 sticks) butter
1/2	t salt

FOR FROSTING:

1	lb. powdered sugar
1	cup butter (2 sticks) butter
1	t vanilla extract
1	T coconut cream
2	cups coconut, toasted (for outside of cake)

Preheat oven to 350 degrees F. Grease two 9 inch round cake pans and set aside. In large bowl, combine cake mix and milk. With hand mixer, beat in eggs, coconut cream, salt and extracts. Microwave butter, sugar and coconut for 4 minutes, stirring halfway through. Add to cake mixture and beat until batter is fully incorporated. Pour batter evenly into cake pans. Bake for 35 minutes or until toothpick inserted into center of cakes comes out clean. Allow cakes to cool. **For Frosting:** In large mixing bowl, beat butter, vanilla extract and coconut cream together. Continue mixing and add powdered sugar. Beat until creamy. Using spatula, coat frosting on top of one cake. Place second cake on top of frosting. Coat entire cake with frosting. Sprinkle top and sides of cake with toasted coconut. Serves 10-12.

For Recipe Photography
& Entertaining Tips, Log onto...

FundaMENUS.COM

_Funda_MENU ❷
Ode to the _Pig_

Salad Course
Sauteed Watercress Salad

☯

Soup Course
Navy Bean & Ham Soup

☯

Main Course
Marinated Pork Loin with Wilted Spinach

☯

Dessert Course
Roasted Banana Bread Pudding

Sauteed Watercress Salad

2	bunches watercress, roughly chopped
2	T sesame oil
2	T garlic, minced
1	T fish sauce
2	bunches fresh spinach, chopped
1/2	cup sesame seeds
1	t salt
1	t black pepper

In frying pan, lightly toast sesame seeds. Remove from pan and set aside. In same pan, saute watercress in oil with garlic, fish sauce and half of the spinach. In large salad bowl, toss uncooked spinach and sesame seeds with sauteed watercress and spinach mixture. Season with salt and pepper. Serve immediately. Serves 12.

Navy Bean & Ham Soup

1	cup yellow onion, chopped
4	T butter
1	cup celery, chopped finely
4	cups ham, cooked & diced
1/4	cup Worcestershire sauce
1	T seasoned salt
1	box chicken broth
1	t black pepper
8	cups cooked navy beans, drained
4	cups water
2	large tomatoes, diced
1/8	cup parsley, dried

In large stock pot, saute onions, celery and ham in butter. Add remaining ingredients to pot and simmer on stove top for 1 hour. Serves 12.

Marinated Pork Lion with Wilted Spinach

For Pork Loin:
2	pork tenderloins
2	T minced garlic
1/2	cup soy sauce
1/4	cup fish sauce
1/4	cup sesame oil
2	t ground ginger
1	t wasabi powder

For Wilted Spinach:
2	large bunches of spinach, roughly chopped
	Brine from pork in zip lock bag after pork has been removed

Remove pork loins from packaging and place in 1 gallon zip lock bag. Add remaining ingredients into bag. Seal and refrigerate overnight. Preheat oven to 350 degrees F. Place tenderloins onto greased cookie sheet. Bake for 25-30 minutes. Take out of oven while center of loins are still pink inside. Let stand 10 minutes before slicing. **For Wilted Spinach:** Pour contents of zip lock bag into large saucepan over medium heat. Cook for 10 minutes. Add spinach, reduce heat and cover for five minutes, incorporating sauce with spinach. Remove spinach from saucepan. Slice pork loin and plate with spinach. Spoon remaining sauce over pork and serve. Serves 12.

Roasted Banana Bread Pudding

1	loaf French Brioche bread, torn
2	t vanilla extract
4	cups whole milk
4	bananas, roasted & mashed
6	eggs
1/2	cup sugar
4	T butter, softened
2	t cinnamon
1	t nutmeg
1	t ginger
1	t pumpkin pie spice
1/2	t salt

Preheat oven to 350 degrees F. Coat 4" x 8" tube pan with cooking spray. In large mixing bowl, tear bread into pieces. Set aside. Place bananas, (skins on) on cookie sheet and bake in oven for 20 minutes. Remove from oven and allow to cool. In medium saucepan over low heat, melt butter and sugar. Stir constantly with wire whisk. Add cinnamon, nutmeg, ginger, pumpkin pie spice and salt. Slowly add milk, stirring constantly. Beat eggs into mixture, stirring constantly. When mixture starts to thicken, remove from heat and cool slightly. Stir in vanilla. Squeeze bananas with peels on, allowing juice to collect into custard mixture. Unpeel bananas and mash with fork in small bowl. Stir into custard mixture. With spatula, pour custard mixture into torn bread pieces. Coat bread with mixture and pour into prepared, tube pan. Place in oven and bake for 30 minutes, until top is golden brown. Serve warm. Serves 12.

FundaMENU ③
Avocado Adventure

Salad Course
Cilantro Avocado Salad with Lime Vinaigrette

☾

Soup Course
Seafood Curry Stew

☾

Main Course
Sesame Tuna Ceviche with Fried Avocados

☾

Dessert Course
Lime & Avocado Cheesecake

Cilantro Avocado Salad with Lime Vinaigrette

4	avocados, peeled, pitted & diced
3	Roma tomatoes, diced
1/2	small onion, finely chopped
1	large seedless cucumber, peeled and diced
1	head Romaine lettuce, torn
1	bunch fresh cilantro, chopped

For Lime Vinaigrette:

1	t black pepper
1/2	t sea salt
1/4	cup lime juice
1/4	cup white wine vinegar
2	T olive oil

In large salad bowl, tear lettuce and combine with avocados, tomatoes, onion, cucumbers and cilantro. **For Lime Vinaigrette:** In separate bowl, whisk together lime juice, vinegar, olive oil, salt and pepper. Set aside. Just before serving, combine lime vinaigrette with salad. Makes 12 servings.

Spicy Seafood Curry Stew

1/2	lb. shrimp, peeled & cut in half
1/2	lb. calamari, cut into rings
1/2	lb. imitation crab meat, flaked
1	whiting filet, cubed
2	T butter
2	T Durkee six pepper seasoning
1	T garlic, minced
1	14 oz. can coconut cream
1	14 oz. can coconut milk
1/2	cup soy sauce
2	T fish sauce
1	cup milk
2	cups water
3	T curry powder
3	T basil, dried
1	T ginger, ground
1	T tarragon, finely chopped

In large stock pot on medium heat, saute shrimp, calamari and whiting cubes in butter and six pepper seasoning. Add remaining ingredients to pot. Reduce heat and simmer for 30-40 minutes, stirring every few minutes. Serves 12.

Sesame Tuna Ceviche

3	lbs. medium grade boneless tuna filets, diced
2	cloves garlic, finely chopped
1/4	cup soy sauce
1/2	cup lime juice
1/4	cup sesame oil
1/2	cup yellow onion, diced
1	cup fresh cilantro, chopped
1/2	t sea salt
1	t black pepper
2	large tomatoes, diced

Dice tuna and place in 1 gallon zip lock bag. Add remaining ingredients and seal bag. Place in refrigerator overnight. Serve cold on top of fried avocado half. Serves 12.

Fried Avocados

6	avocados, peeled, pitted & halved
2	cups Italian seasoned bread crumbs
3	eggs, beaten
4	cups corn oil (for frying)

Heat oil in small saucepan. Dip avocados in egg and dredge in bread crumbs. When oil is ready, place avocados gently in oil, two at a time. Fry until golden brown and remove and drain from oil. Place on paper towels to absorb excess oil. Place on cookie sheet and place in oven at 200 degrees until ready to serve. **Note:** Best served within an hour of frying. Serves 12.

Lime & Avocado Cheesecake

For Crust:
2	cups vanilla wafers, crushed
1/2	t vanilla extract
3	T butter, melted
2	T sugar

For Filling:
1.5	8 oz. packages cream cheese, softened
1	t vanilla extract
3/4	cup sugar
2	ripe avocados, mashed
3	eggs
1/4	cup lime juice
1	T grated lime zest

For Topping:
4	T butter, softened
4	ozs. cream cheese, softened
1/2	lb. powdered sugar
1	T grated lime zest
1	t vanilla

Preheat oven to 350 degrees F. Grease large springform pan. **For Crust:** In a medium bowl, combine graham cracker crumbs, sugar, vanilla extract and butter. Press the crust evenly into the bottom and sides of springform pan. Place in oven and bake for 10 minutes. Remove crust from oven and cool. Reduce oven heat to 325 degrees F. **For Filling:** In large bowl, using hand mixer, beat cream cheese, vanilla and sugar. Beat thoroughly. Add eggs one at a time, mashed avocado, lime juice and zest. Beat until smooth. Pour filling into crust. Place aluminum foil around outside of springform pan and put pan into sheet cake pan filled with one inch of water. Place pans in oven and bake for 55 minutes. Turn off oven and leave cheese-cake in the oven for 20 minutes or until the center is firm to touch. Cool slightly. **For Topping:** In medium bowl using hand mixer, beat together cream cheese, butter and zest. Slowly beat in powdered sugar until smooth and creamy. Place topping in pastry bag and pipe onto top of cheesecake. Serves 12-16.

FundaMENU ④
All American Meal

Salad Course
Rosemary & Potato Salad

☙

Soup Course
Cream of Stilton & Cauliflower Soup

☙

Main Course
Beef Tenderloin with Stilton Butter Sauce & Fingerling Potatoes

☙

Dessert Course
Chocolate Fudge Pie

Rosemary & Potato Salad

1	bunch Romaine lettuce, torn
2	large potatoes, peeled & diced
1	small onion, chopped
1	3 oz. container Feta cheese
1	cup Craisins
1	t black pepper
1	t seasoned salt
2	T olive oil
2	T rosemary, dried
3/4	cup Balsamic Vinaigrette dressing
1	cup carrots, grated
	juice from half a lemon
3	cups croutons

In frying pan, over medium heat, cook potatoes with olive oil, rosemary, seasoning salt, pepper and onion. Remove from heat. In salad bowl, mix salad greens with craisins, cheese and carrots. Add warm potatoes. Toss quickly with dressing. Squeeze with lemon juice, season with salt and pepper, add croutons and serve immediately. Serves 12.

Cream of Stilton & Cauliflower Soup

1	head cauliflower, roughly chopped
1	stick margarine
3/4	cup yellow onion, chopped
2	chicken base
4	cups water (for soup)
6	cups water (for cauliflower)
3	small cans cream of potato soup
1/3	bunch fresh tarragon, chopped
1/8	cup fresh parsley, chopped
1	cup milk
3	cups heavy cream
2	t nutmeg
1 1/2	t celery salt
1	cup celery, chopped
2	t garlic, chopped
2	t black pepper
6	ozs. Stilton blue cheese, crumbled

Fill large pot with water and bring to boil. Add cauliflower and cook until very tender. Drain and set aside. In another large pot, saute celery, onions and garlic with margarine. Add remaining ingredients. Simmer for 1 hour, stirring every few minutes. Remove from heat and boat motor for 5 minutes until smooth. Makes 12 large servings.

Beef Tenderloin with Stilton Butter Sauce

1	3 lb. beef tenderloin roast
1/2	cup Worcestershire sauce
3	cloves garlic, chopped
1	t white pepper

For Stilton Butter Sauce:

1	stick butter
1	3 oz. package Stilton blue cheese, crumbled

Place beef into one gallon zip lock bag. Add Worcestershire sauce, garlic and white pepper. Refrigerate overnight. Preheat oven to 350 degrees F. Place roast into a shallow, glass baking dish. Pour brine over beef. Bake in preheated oven for 10 minutes, then turn the roast over, and continue cooking 35 to 40 minutes, basting occasionally until desired doneness (140 degrees F for medium rare). Let meat rest for 10 to 15 minutes before slicing. **For Stilton Butter Sauce:** While beef is resting, melt butter in small saucepan. Reduce heat and stir in Stilton. Top sliced beef with sauce. Serves 12.

Roasted Fingerling Potatoes

3   lbs. fingerling potatoes, cut in half, lengthwise
3   T sesame oil
2   cloves garlic, chopped

Preheat oven to 400 degrees F. Mix potatoes with oil and garlic in large bowl. Place potatoes on greased cookie sheet and bake for 50 minutes, turning halfway through baking process. Remove of oven and serve with beef tenderloin. Serves 12.

Chocolate Fudge Pie

2	pie crusts

For Filling:

3	sticks butter
3	cups chocolate chips, melted
5	large eggs
1 3/4	cups sugar
1 1/4	cups flour
1	T vanilla
1	cup chopped walnuts
1/2	t cayenne pepper

For Topping:

1	stick butter
2	cups chocolate morsels
1	t vanilla
1/2	lb. powdered sugar
1	small container whipped topping (for top of pies)

Preheat oven to 300 degrees F. **For Filling:** Melt butter and chocolate chips in microwave. In large bowl, mix together remaining ingredients (except nuts) with hand mixer for 5 minutes. Stir in nuts. Pour batter into pie crusts. Place in oven and bake for 40 minutes. Remove from oven and cool completely. **For Topping:** Melt butter & morsels in microwave. Mix in remaining ingredients using hand mixer. Cover cooled pies with topping. Top each pie with whipped cream. Garnish with shaved chocolate if desired. Serves 16.

For Recipe Photography
& Entertaining Tips, Log onto...

*Funda*MENUS.COM

*Funda*MENU ⑤

Taste of Tuscany

Salad Course
Feta, Mint & Couscous Salad

☾

Soup Course
Quick & Creamy Tomato Basil Soup

☾

Main Course
Spinach & Artichoke Lasagna with Garlic Bread

☾

Dessert Course
Southern Style Cream Cake

Feta, Mint & Couscous Salad

2	cups water
1	lb. couscous
1/4	cup Balsamic vinegar
1/4	cup lemon juice
1/4	cup white vinegar
3	seedless cucumbers, cubed into 1/2 inch chunks
1/2	cup shelled pistachios
1/2	bag radishes, sliced
1/2	bunch fresh mint, chopped
1	3 oz. container Feta cheese, crumbled
1/2	t sea salt
1	t black pepper

In medium pot, boil water on high heat. Add couscous, turn heat down to low, cover and simmer for 5 minutes. Fluff couscous with fork. Remove from heat and allow to cool. In large bowl, combine all ingredients except for pistachios and radishes. Refrigerate salad and just before serving, stir in pistachios and radishes.
Makes 12 servings.

Quick & Creamy Tomato Basil Soup

3	lbs. crushed tomatoes
2	small cans cream of tomato soup
1/2	quart heavy cream
1/2	quart whole milk
1	T salt
1	T black pepper
1	bunch basil, finely chopped
1/2	cup sugar

Place all ingredients into large stock pot. Cook for 1 hour on low heat, stirring occasionally. Remove from heat. Using electric boat motor, blend until smooth. Serves 12.

Spinach & Artichoke Lasagna

For Sauce:

1/2	cup onion, chopped
2	T butter
1/2	cup green bell peppers, chopped
1	can (1 lb.) crushed tomatoes
1	can (1 lb.) diced tomatoes
1	can (1 lb. 10oz) Marinara sauce
1	can (1 lb.) sliced mushrooms, drained
1/2	cup Parmesan cheese, grated
1.5	T chopped garlic
1/4	cup dried basil
1/4	cup dried oregano
1	T black pepper
1/2	T salt

For Filling:

1.5	lbs. frozen spinach, thawed
1	lb ricotta cheese
1	lb cottage cheese
1	1 lb. can artichokes, drained
1/2	cup Parmesan cheese
1	small package Ranch dressing

For Assembly:

2	packages (12 noodles per box) Lasagna noodles, uncooked
3/4	cups Parmesan cheese
1.5	cups Monterey Jack cheese
	fresh oregano, for sprinkling
	fresh parsley, for sprinkling

For Sauce: In large pot, melt butter. Add onions, peppers, garlic and spices. Add remaining ingredients, stirring often. Cook on low heat for 30 minutes. **For Filling:** In large bowl mix together filling ingredients. Set aside. Preheat oven to 350 degrees F.

For Assembly: Cover bottom of large casserole dish with sauce. Place 4 noodles on top of sauce. Repeat two times. Spoon spinach mixture onto noodles and sauce. Repeat with sauce and noodles twice and spoon spinach mixture on top. End with a layer of noodles and top with sauce. Add cheeses. Sprinkle with more oregano and parsley. Cover casserole dish with aluminum foil. Place in oven for 1 1/2 hours or until noodles are tender. Cut to make 12 equally-sized portions. Serve with garlic bread. Serves 12.

Garlic Bread

1	loaf Italian bread, cut into twelve, thick slices
1	stick butter, melted
1	T minced garlic
1/2	cup fresh Parmesan cheese, grated

Preheat oven to 350 degrees F. Grease cookie sheet with garlic oil. Place bread slices on cookie sheet. In small bowl, combine butter and garlic. Brush both sides of bread with butter mixture. Sprinkle cheese evenly on top of bread. Place in oven for 15 minutes until bread turns golden brown. Serve with spinach & artichoke lasagna. Serves 12.

Southern Style Cream Cake

For Batter:

1	cup butter, softened
5	egg yolks
5	egg whites
1	t baking soda
1	t vanilla extract
2	cups sugar
2	cups flour
1 1/2	cups buttermilk
1	cup walnuts, finely chopped
1	cup sweetened coconut, flaked

For Cream Cheese Icing:

16	ozs. cream cheese, softened
1	cup (2 sticks) butter
7	cups powdered sugar
1	t pure vanilla extract

Preheat oven to 350 degrees F. Grease three 9 inch square cake pans and set aside. **For Batter:** Cream together butter, egg yolks and sugar with hand mixer. Add remaining ingredients except for egg whites and mix until creamy. In separate bowl, beat egg whites with hand mixer until it forms a meringue. Fold egg whites into cake mixture. Pour mixture evenly into 3 cake pans. Place in oven and bake for 25 minutes. Allow cakes to cool. **For Cream Cheese Icing:** With hand mixer, in large bowl, cream butter and cream cheese. Mix in remaining ingredients until smooth and creamy. Top one cake layer with cream cheese icing. Place second cake square on top and coat with cream cheese frosting. Place third cake square on top of cake squares and coat entire three-layer cake with icing. Serves 12-20, depending on size preferences.

FundaMENU ⑥

Mexican Fiesta

Salad Course
Black Bean & Hominy Salad

☾

Soup Course
Chorizo & Black Bean Soup

☾

Main Course
Black Bean Burritos with Jalapeno Corn Bread

☾

Dessert Course
Cayenne Pepper Chocolate Squares

Black Bean & Hominy Salad

1	large head red leaf lettuce, torn
1	small can black beans, drained
1	small can hominy, drained
2	Roma tomatoes, diced
1/2	cup purple onion, sliced thin
1	cup fresh cilantro, chopped
1/4	cup jalapeno peppers, chopped
1	t sea salt
1/2	cup Creamy Cucumber salad dressing
2	T olive oil

Place oil in large frying pan over medium heat. Saute hominy in pan until golden brown. Place remaining ingredients into large salad bowl. Add hominy and toss with cucumber salad dressing just before serving. Serves 12.

Chorizo & Black Bean Soup

1	lb. Chorizo
1/2	cup yellow onion, diced
6	Roma tomatoes, diced
4	cloves garlic, chopped
2	T butter
2	T Cajun seasoning
2	small cans black beans, with juice
2	t hot sauce
1	small can yellow corn, with juice
3/4	cup fresh cilantro, chopped
	juice from 1 lime
3	cups water
	tortilla chips, for garnish

Place butter in frying pan over medium heat. Add onion, garlic and Chorizo. Cook until Chorizo is brown and onions are caramelized. Drain and set aside. In large stock pot, over medium heat, combine tomatoes, corn, beans and hot sauce. Add Chorizo mixture to pot with remaining ingredients. Reduce heat and simmer for 40 minutes, stirring every ten minutes. Place into small bowls and garnish with tortilla chips. Serves 12.

Black Bean Burritos

2.5	cups cooked rice
2	small cans black beans, drained
1	small can yellow corn, drained
1/2	cup green chilies
1/2	T black pepper
1/2	T seasoned salt
1	T cumin
1/2	cup Enchilada sauce (for mixture)
1/2	cup diced red peppers
1/2	T minced garlic
1/2	cup diced green peppers
1/4	cup yellow onion, diced
2	cups Cheddar cheese, shredded
2	cups Monterey Jack cheese, shredded
12	flour tortillas
3	cups Enchilada sauce, (for bottom and top of casserole dish)

Preheat oven to 350 degrees F. In large bowl, combine all ingredients, saving 1 cup of Jack cheese and 1 cup Cheddar cheese for topping. Place unopened package of flour tortillas in microwave for 35 seconds. Remove from package and fill center of each flour tortilla with mixture. Fold both ends of tortilla into itself and roll rest of tortilla enclosing mixture inside. Place 1.5 cups of sauce in bottom of large casserole dish. Place 12 Enchiladas in casserole dish. Cover Enchiladas with remaining Enchilada sauce and cheeses. Cover casserole dish with aluminum foil and bake for 40 minutes until heated through. Serves 12.

Spicy Jalapeno Corn Bread

1	8.5 ounce package corn bread mix
1/2	cup yellow corn from can, drained
1	t salt
1/2	cup buttermilk
1	egg, beaten
1/4	cup green chilies
2	t cayenne pepper
1	cup Cheddar cheese, shredded

Preheat oven to 400 degrees F. In large mixing bowl, using hand mixer, combine all ingredients. Pour mixture into a greased, square, casserole dish. Bake for 15-20 minutes or until a wooden pick inserted in center comes out clean. Cool in pan 10 minutes on a wire rack. Cut into squares. Serves 12.

Cayenne Pepper Chocolate Squares

For Mixture:

1/2	cup flour
1	cup walnuts, chopped
2	eggs, lightly beaten
3/4	cup butter, melted
6	T cocoa powder
1	t cinnamon
1	cup light brown sugar
1	t vanilla extract
3/4	t cayenne pepper

For Topping:

4	ozs. semisweet chocolate chips
2	T butter
1	T sour cream
1	t cinnamon

Preheat oven to 350 degrees F. Grease 8 inch square cake pan. **For Mixture:** In large mixing bowl, using hand mixer, beat butter and cocoa together. Beat in eggs, sugar and vanilla extract. Gradually mix in flour, cinnamon and cayenne pepper. Stir in nuts. Pour mixture into cake pan and bake for 20-35 minutes until risen. Remove from oven and allow to cool. **For Topping:** In small bowl, combine butter and chocolate. Place in microwave on high for 30 second intervals, stirring after each interval. Heat until chocolate melts completely. Stir in sour cream and cinnamon. Using hand mixer, beat until smooth and glossy. Allow to cool and pour mixture evenly over brownies and cut into squares. Serves 12-16.

For Recipe Photography
& Entertaining Tips, Log onto...

FundaMENUS.COM

FundaMENU 7

Comfort Food Fusion

Salad Course
Pickled Beet & Goat Cheese Salad

❦

Soup Course
Potato & Parsnip Soup

❦

Main Course
Meat Loaf with Tomato Chutney & Rosemary Creamed Corn

❦

Dessert Course
Cinnamon Pineapple Upside Down Cake

Pickled Beet & Goat Cheese Salad

1	bunch spinach, chopped
1	small can pickled beets, drained and diced
1/2	cup walnuts, chopped
3	ozs. goat cheese, sliced
1	cup golden raisins
1	t sea salt
1	t black pepper
1/2	cup Balsamic Vinaigrette dressing

In large salad bowl, mix spinach with walnuts, raisins, salt and pepper. Cover and place in refrigerator until ready to serve. Toss with dressing and stir in goat cheese and beets. Serves 12.

Potato & Parsnip Soup

4	T butter
3	T fresh rosemary, chopped
1	lb. frozen yellow corn
3	small cans Cream of Potato soup
3	cups water (for soup)
1	large parsnip, peeled & diced
3	cups water (for parsnips)
1	t salt
1	T black pepper

Place parsnip in 3 cups of boiling water. Cook until very tender. Drain & set aside. Place butter in large stockpot over medium heat. Add rosemary and corn after butter melts. Stir in remaining ingredients, (including parsnips) and turn heat to low. Simmer for 30 minutes, stirring every few minutes. Remove from heat and using an electric boat motor, mix until smooth and creamy. Place in small bowls and garnish with rosemary. Serves 12.

Meat Loaf with Tomato Chutney

For Mixture:
3	lbs. ground beef
6	eggs
1/4	cup Worcestershire sauce
6	slices white bread, torn
1	small packet onion soup mix
1/2	cup ketchup
1/2	cup yellow onion, finely chopped
1	t salt
1	t black pepper

For Tomato Chutney:
1	large tomato, diced
1	small can crushed tomatoes
1	medium yellow onion, chopped
1	large green bell pepper
2	T ketchup
2	T sugar
1	t salt
1	t black pepper
1	t hot sauce

Preheat oven to 350 degrees F. **For Mixture:** In large bowl, mix ground beef with all mixture ingredients. Place mixture into casserole dish. Using hands, pat meat loaf firmly into casserole dish. Using hands, make a line down the center of the dish and shape mixture into two loaves. Place in oven and bake for one hour or until done in center. Remove from heat and drain. Allow to stand 10 minutes before cutting into slices. **For Tomato Chutney:** In large saucepan on medium heat, cook onions and bell peppers. Add tomatoes and remaining ingredients and cook until mixture starts to bubble. Stir often. Remove from heat and spoon generously onto Meat loaf. Serves 12.

Rosemary Creamed Corn

1/2	stick butter
2	pinches kosher salt
10	ears fresh corn, shucked & cut off the cob
1/2	cup vegetable shortening
1/4	cup fresh rosemary, chopped
3	T sugar
2	cups milk
1/2	cup flour
1	t black pepper

In large mixing bowl, place a cutting board in the middle of the bowl. Cut cob in a vertical position and remove only the tops of the kernel with a knife, using long, smooth downward strokes and rotating the cob as needed. After e cob has been stripped, use dull backside of the knife to scrape any remaining pulp and milk off of cob. In large saucepan, heat shortening and salt on high heat until it is hot enough for frying. Add corn mixed with sugar to the saucepan and cook over medium high until corn changes texture. Add butter and cover with milk, pepper and rosemary after butter melts. When milk starts to froth, add flour using a sifter, stirring constantly. When corn thickens remove from heat. Garnish with rosemary and serve. Serves 12.

Cinnamon Pineapple Upside Down Cake

For Batter:
1	18.5 oz. box yellow cake mix
1 1/2	cups pineapple juice
1	t vanilla
1/2	cup crushed pineapple
1	t cinnamon

For Topping:
1	cup brown sugar
1	cup chopped walnuts
1	t cinnamon
1	stick butter
2	cups crushed pineapple
	Maraschino cherries, for garnish

Preheat oven to 350 degrees F. Using hand mixer, combine all batter ingredients. Set aside. **For Topping:** Prepare topping by placing sugar and butter in a microwave on high for three minutes. Stir in remaining ingredients. Grease two round cake pans and divide topping mixture evenly between pans. Pour cake batter over topping. Bake for 40 minutes. Let cool slightly and flip over one cake pan onto serving plate. Place second cake onto first cake. Garnish with sliced Maraschino cherries and serve. Serves 12-16.

For Recipe Photography
& Entertaining Tips, Log onto...

*Funda*MENUS.COM

*Funda*MENUS

Chapter 8

Appeteasing Appetizers

 hen hosting a dinner party, one of the most important things to have in anyone's recipe arsenal is a flavorful and original appetizer. After all, appetizers set the tone of every dinner party engagement and the first bite gives the guest a teasing taste of what flavors they can expect throughout the evening. That is why I have created seven, intensely flavorful first bites that will be the hit of any dinner gathering.

Each appetizer works well with any of the themed **FundaMENUS** that I have created for this book, but I have given my personal recommendations of which appetizers pair best with every **FundaMENU**, so they can really shine. These appetizers can also be substituted or added to any of the budget-friendly buffet **FundaMENUS** for larger crowds. And best of all, the recipes can be used together for an unforgettable appetizer-themed dinner party.

*Funda*MENU ⑧

Appeteasing Appetizers

Stilton, Bacon & Walnut Cheese Balls

❦

Salmon Cakes with Cucumber Dill Sauce

❦

Miso Dip with Fennel, Cucumbers & Carrots

❦

Coconut Chicken Bites with Honey-Coconut Dipping Sauce

❦

Balsamic & Basil Stuffed Mushrooms

❦

Mexican Ravioli

❦

Fried Bacon, Macaroni & Cheese Fritters

Stilton, Bacon & Walnut Cheese Balls

For Mixture:

6	ozs. Stilton blue cheese
8	ozs. cream cheese
1/2	cup chopped walnuts
1/2	cup bacon, cooked & chopped

For Coating:

1	cup Graham crackers, finely chopped in food processor
2	t sugar
1	T melted butter

For Mixture: In large bowl, mix cheeses together with hands. Add bacon and walnuts, mixing thoroughly. Set aside. **For Coating:** In smaller bowl, mix Graham crackers, sugar and melted butter. Roll cheese mixture into 1 inch balls and dredge into cracker mixture. Place on platter, cover and refrigerate until ready to serve. Makes 2 dozen balls.

*Funda*MENU *Recommendation*

Ode to the Pig

Salmon Cakes with Cucumber Dill Sauce

For Mixture:
2	14.75 oz. cans salmon, picked
3/4	cup yellow onion, diced
1 1/2	cups celery (4 stalks), diced
1/2	cup red bell pepper, diced
1/2	cup green bell pepper, diced
1/4	cup sour cream
2	T lemon juice
1	cup herb stuffing mix
1/4	cup mayonnaise
2	T Caribbean jerk seasoning
2	large eggs,lightly beaten
1/2	cup onion, diced
2	T butter, melted
1/2	t salt
1/2	t pepper
	olive oil for frying

For Cucumber Dill Sauce:
1/2	cup sour cream
1/4	cup mayonnaise
1/4	cup yellow onion, finely chopped
1/4	cup fresh dill, finely chopped
1/2	cup cucumber, peeled & diced
1	T lemon juice

For Mixture: In large bowl, combine salmon, onion, sour cream, lemon juice, herb stuffing mix, mayonnaise, eggs and seasonings. In small bowl, melt butter in microwave. Add celery and bell peppers to butter. Cover with plastic wrap and microwave for 5 minutes, stirring halfway through. Place mixture into salmon mixture and mix thoroughly. With hands, shape 24 patties out of mixture. In large skillet, heat oil on high heat. Fry salmon cakes in batches, cooking each side for 4 minutes. When golden brown remove from heat and place on paper towel to drain off remaining oil. **For Cucumber Dill Sauce:** In small bowl, combine all ingredients, stirring with wire whisk. Dollop sauce on each salmon cake and serve. Makes 24 small, salmon cakes.

*Funda*MENU Recommendation

Asian Inspiration

Miso Dip with Fennel, Cucumbers & Carrots

1	T sesame oil
2	T rice vinegar
3	T Miso
2	cloves garlic
1	jalapeno pepper
1	bunch of fresh cilantro
3/4	cup olive oil

For Vegetable Platter:

1	seedless cucumber, sliced
1	small package baby carrots
1	bulb fennel, chopped into pieces

Place all above ingredients except olive oil and cilantro in food processor, then slowly add olive oil while pulsing. Blend on high while adding cilantro. Process until smooth. Makes approximately 3 cups of dip. Serve with fennel, baby carrots and seedless cucumbers. Serves 12.

*Funda*MENU *Recommendation*

Avocado Adventure

Coconut Chicken Bites
with Honey-Coconut Dipping Sauce

For Brine:

5	lbs. raw chicken breasts, cut into nugget-sized pieces
1	8 oz. can of coconut milk
1	8 oz. can of coconut cream
3/4	cup Dijon mustard

For Coating:

1	stick margarine, melted
4	cups Italian bread crumbs

For Dipping Sauce:

1/2	8 oz. can coconut cream
1/2	8 oz. can coconut milk
1/4	cup honey

For Brine: In large zip lock bag, place cubed chicken, coconut milk, coconut cream and Dijon mustard. Coat thoroughly and refrigerate overnight. Preheat oven to 350 degrees F. **For Coating:** Melt margarine in microwave. Mix in bread crumbs. Take chicken cubes out of refrigerator and roll in bread crumbs and place on a greased cookie sheet. Bake in oven for 25-30 minutes until crispy. **For Dipping Sauce:** In small bowl, add all ingredients and whisk. Makes about 2 cups. Serves 12.

FundaMENU Recommendation

All American Meal

Balsamic & Basil Stuffed Mushrooms

1	large package button mushrooms
1	bunch fresh basil, leaves only
1	T minced garlic
1/2	cup Balsamic vinegar
1	cup Marinara sauce
1	cup Mozzarella cheese, grated
1	t black pepper

Preheat oven to 350 degrees F. Clean and remove stems from mushrooms and place tops onto cookie sheet. Brush each mushroom cap with balsamic vinegar. Season with pepper and garlic. Place a basil leaf on each mushroom cap. Add Marinara sauce on top, followed by cheese. Place in oven and bake for 15 minutes. Remove from oven and serve. Serves 12-16.

*Funda*MENU *Recommendation*

Taste of Tuscany

Mexican Ravioli

For Dough:
3 cups flour
3 eggs
1/4 cup water
1 t olive oil

For Filling:
1/2 lb. ground beef
1/4 cup fresh cilantro, chopped
1/2 yellow onion, diced
2 t hot sauce
1 t black pepper
2 T Worcestershire sauce
1 t seasoned salt
1 cup Cheddar cheese
1 cup corn oil, for frying

For Dough: Place flour in large bowl. Make a well in the center of the flour. Beat in eggs with fork. Gradually add water and oil. Stir together, forming a ball. Turn onto a floured surface and knead until smooth and dough becomes elastic. Cover and allow to rest for 30 minutes. Roll dough to 1/16 inch thickness. Cut out 48 circles using a biscuit cutter.

For Filling: In large frying pan, saute beef, onion, hot sauce, salt and pepper. Drain grease from beef after cooking. Stir in remaining ingredients. Place one tablespoon of mixture into center of 24 circles. Add a small amount of moisture to circumference of circles. Place remaining circles on top of mixture. Press each ravioli together using fingers and seal with prongs of fork. Place ravioli on floured cookie sheet and refrigerate for 30 minutes. Heat oil in frying pan. Place 6 to 8 ravioli in oil and fry both sides until brown. Place fried ravioli on paper towels to absorb excess oil. Place ravioli back on cookie sheet and place into oven on warm until ready to serve. Makes 24 ravioli. Serves 12.

FundaMENU Recommendation

Mexican Fiesta

Fried Bacon, Macaroni & Cheese Fritters

1	11 oz. can Pillsbury Refrigerated Crusty French Loaf
1	lb. store bought macaroni and cheese from local deli
1	lb. bacon, cooked & chopped
4	cups corn oil, for frying

Cook bacon in frying pan per package directions. Drain bacon and place on paper towels to absorb excess oil. Allow to cool and cut bacon into small pieces and place into large bowl. Mix in macaroni and cheese. With damp hands, form 24 small balls. Carefully unroll French loaf onto large cutting board. Cut dough into 24 squares. Place macaroni ball into center of each dough piece. Completely cover dough around macaroni ball, making sure there are no holes. In small sauce pan, heat oil. Drop 4 to 5 balls into hot oil and fry until golden brown. Place fried fritters on paper towels to absorb excess oil. Place in oven on warm until ready to serve. **Note:** Fritters are best served within an hour of frying. Makes 24 fritters. Serves 12.

FundaMENU Recommendation

Comfort Food Fusion

For Recipe Photography
& Entertaining Tips, Log onto...

*Funda*MENUS.COM

*Funda*MENUS

Chapters 9-11
Budget-Friendly Buffets

I f preparing a four-course dinner doesn't work within your party plans because of a large number of guests, then why not choose to set up an elaborate buffet instead? Buffets for social gatherings are easier to prepare ahead of time and in most cases, they are often more affordable than a smaller sit-down dinner party. By adding a few new quick and affordable recipes provided within the following chapters, hosting an amazing, upscale dinner buffet can be within anyone's reach. I have provided three, thoughtfully-themed buffet menus that can be used for any occasion. The menus can also be easily modified by swapping out some of the recipes with other recipes mentioned within the **FundaMENUS** chapters within this book, for four-course dinner parties.

To assist in preparing the ultimate buffet, I have also included tips on how to present the recipes on a buffet so it will appear to have been prepared by a high-end caterer. In order to pull off a successful buffet party for a large number of guests, make sure not to get fixated by the number of people that are on the guest list. Rather, focus your energies on a "one recipe at a time" mentality so your next buffet dinner party will be a show-stopper achieved with minimal effort.

A **FundaMENU** for a formal buffet requires three, basic, fundamental ingredients...**Savory Appetizers**, **Sinfully Sweet Desserts** and most importantly, a **Killer Cocktail**. When preparing my menus for a buffet for 50 guests, make sure to offer at least five savory dishes, three desserts and one specialty cocktail for each buffet scenario. A more experienced cook can handle a more extensive buffet menu, but in actuality, preparing eight recipes and creating one specialty cocktail for a dinner party is more than enough variety for your guests, as long as the recipes on the buffet are flavorful and are visually appealing.

For Recipe Photography
& Entertaining Tips, Log onto...

FundaMENUS.COM

FundaMENU 9
French Fundamentals

Lemon Pepper Chicken Tenders

☾

Cilantro Pork Sliders

☾

Cheese Fondue with Brioche & Pears

☾

Vidalia Onion Tartlets

☾

Apricot Cheese Puffs

☾

Cinnamon Figs with Cognac Cream

☾

Rice Pudding Shots

☾

Cayenne Chocolate Covered Strawberry Bouquet

Lemon Pepper Chicken Tenders

5   lbs. boneless chicken breasts, cut into thin strips
3   T lemon pepper seasoning
1   cup lemon juice
1   T seasoned salt
4   T butter

Place strips of chicken into large zip lock bag with all ingredients except for butter. Seal and shake ingredients together in bag and place in refrigerator overnight. Remove chicken from bag, set aside juice and place chicken in large frying pan over medium heat with butter. Saute chicken in batches until chicken is just undercooked. Pour juice over chicken and cook until chicken is fully cooked. Remove from heat and place into heated chaffing dish and serve. Serves 40-50.

Cilantro Pork Sliders

3	lbs. ground pork
1/2	cup fresh cilantro, chopped
1/4	cup lemon juice
1/2	cup soy sauce
1/4	cup Worcestershire sauce
1	t white pepper
1	t black pepper
3	eggs
2	cups bread crumbs
1/2	cup Thousand Island dressing
	Freshly chopped cilantro (for garnish)

For Mini Rolls:

1	container refrigerated, Pillsbury French Loaf

Preheat oven to 350 degrees F. Mix together ground pork (except for Thousand Island dressing) with all other ingredients. Roll mixture into 50 small balls and place onto greased, cookie sheet. With hands, pat each ball to form a patty. Cover and refrigerate until ready to use. **For Mini Rolls:** Grease two cookie sheets. Remove packaging from French loaf and roll dough into 50 small balls. Place on cookie sheets and bake for 15 minutes or until bread turns golden brown. Remove from oven and cool. Place meat patties in oven and bake for 30 minutes. Turn off oven and leave patties in oven until ready to assemble sliders. Slice each roll in half. Coat each side of bread with dressing. Place one patty onto base of each roll. Top each patty with cilantro. Cover each patty with top of roll. Quickly insert toothpick into center of each slider to hold in place. Place sliders into heated chaffing dish and serve. Serves 50.

Cheese Fondue with Brioche & Pears

1	lb. Swiss cheese, shredded
1	lb. Gruyere cheese, shredded
4	T cornstarch
2	t minced garlic
2	cups white wine
2	T lemon juice
1	t dry mustard
1	t nutmeg
1	t white pepper

For Dippers:

1	loaf French Brioche, cut into 1 inch cubes
5	pears, cut into slices & tossed in 1/2 cup lime juice

In a small bowl, coat the cheeses with cornstarch and set aside. In large saucepan over medium heat, add wine, garlic and lemon juice and bring to a simmer. Gradually stir cheeses into mixture. Continue stirring and add white pepper & nutmeg. Pour mixture into heated Fondue pot or crock pot. Serve with sliced pears and Brioche with wooden skewers. Serves 50.

Vidalia Onion Tartlets

1	container refrigerated biscuit dough
3	large Vidalia onions, diced
3	T butter
1	8 oz. package cream cheese
1	cup heavy cream
1	t white pepper
1	t sea salt
2	T sugar
1	t nutmeg

Preheat oven to 350 degrees F. Grease bottom and sides of large casserole dish. Cover bottom of dish with biscuit dough and bake for 10 minutes. Remove from oven and set aside. In large frying pan, heat butter on medium heat. Add onions, white pepper, salt, sugar and nutmeg. Cook until onions are caramelized. Reduce heat and stir in cream cheese, (torn) and heavy cream. Cook until mixture is thick and creamy. Pour and spread mixture evenly over half-cooked biscuit dough. Place back into oven for 20 minutes. Remove from oven and cool slightly. Cut into fifty equally-sized pieces and place onto platters. Place into oven (on warm) until ready to serve. Serves 50.

Apricot Cheese Puffs

1	package puff pastry (2 sheets)
1	medium jar apricot preserves
1	8 oz. package cream cheese, softened
1	3 oz. package herb goat cheese, softened
2	jalapeno peppers, seeded and finely chopped

Preheat oven to 375 degrees F. Spray three, 24 count mini muffin pans. **Note:** If you have only 1 muffin pan, assemble pastries and bake in batches. Unroll puff pastry sheets and cut into 72 equally-sized squares. Fill muffin pans with puff pastry sheet to take shape of muffin pan. In mixing bowl, using fork, mix together cream cheese and goat cheese. Drop mixture by 1/2 teaspoons over pastry dough. Spoon apricot preserves by 1/2 teaspoons over cheese mixture. Place pans into oven and bake for 20-25 minutes or until pastry has puffed and turned golden brown. Remove from oven and sprinkle peppers evenly over puffs. Platter puffs and serve at room temperature. Makes 72 cheese puffs.

Cinnamon Figs with Cognac Cream

For Figs:
24	small figs, cut in half
1	T cinnamon
1	T sugar
1	t pumpkin pie spice
3	T butter

For Cinnamon Cognac Cream:
1	small container heavy whipping cream
2	T sugar
1	t vanilla extract
1	t cinnamon
2	T Cognac

For Figs: Preheat oven to 350 degrees F. Place figs in small pot of boiling water. Cook for 10 minutes. Remove from heat and Drain. In small bowl, mix sugar, cinnamon and pumpkin pie spice. Dredge figs in sugar mixture and place onto cookie sheet. Bake in oven for 20 minutes. Remove from heat and cool. **For Cinnamon Cognac Cream:** In mixing bowl, using hand mixer, combine whipping cream and sugar. Beat until mixture starts to thicken. Add remaining ingredients. Beat until mixture is fluffy and creamy. Place cream into pastry bag and pipe onto baked figs. Place on platter and serve. Makes 48 tarts.

Rice Pudding Shots

3	cups white rice
8	cups water
6	cups milk
2	cups sugar
2	t salt
2	eggs, beaten
2	cups golden raisins
4	T butter
2	t vanilla extract
4	t cinnamon

In a medium saucepan over high heat, bring water and rice to a boil. Stir. Reduce heat, cover and simmer for 30 minutes. Add 4 cups milk, sugar and salt. Cook over medium heat until thick and creamy, 15 to 20 minutes. Stir in remaining milk, beaten eggs and raisins. Cook 2 minutes more, stirring constantly. Remove from heat, and stir in butter, vanilla and cinnamon. Place into 50 clear, disposable shot glasses and serve with small, wooden tasting spoons. Serves 50.

Cayenne Chocolate Covered Strawberry Bouquet

2	large containers strawberries
2	small containers fudge icing
2	t cayenne pepper
50-60	bamboo skewers
2	blocks green floral foam
1	large-mouthed and wide-based, opaque vase

Cut 1 block of floral foam to fit snugly inside vase of choice. Place the other foam block onto a sheet of wax paper. Place strawberries, (stem first) onto bamboo skewers. Open 1 container of icing and place uncovered into microwave. Melt icing in 15 seconds at a time, stirring between intervals. Add 1 teaspoon of pepper into container and mix thoroughly. Repeat process with icing when the first icing is depleted. Dip each strawberry skewer into chocolate and insert into foam block with wax paper to dry. Once strawberries have hardened slightly, arrange strawberries into vase to form a bouquet. Refrigerate until ready to serve. Place on buffet table and serve. Serves 50.

*Funda*MENU ❿
Classic Concoctions

Ham, Swiss & Poppy Seed Mustard Sliders

☯

Buffalo Chicken Tartlets

☯

Cheesy Chili Dog Bites

☯

Mini Stuffed Dill Potatoes

☯

Three Layer Bean Dip with Blue Corn Tortilla Chips

☯

Chocolate Covered Cake Pops

☯

Chocolate Chocolate Chip Cookies

☯

Peach Cobbler Crescents

Ham, Swiss & Poppy Seed Mustard Sliders

2	11.3 oz. containers refrigerated dinner rolls
1	lb. deli ham, thinly sliced
1	lb. deli Swiss cheese, thinly sliced
1	cup yellow mustard
1/2	cup poppy seeds
1	large yellow onion, diced
1	t black pepper

Preheat oven to 375 degrees F. Grease cookie sheet. Remove dinner rolls from packages and separate. Divide each roll into fourths. Place rolls onto greased cookie sheet and space so 64 rolls fit onto one cookie sheet. **Note:** Allow equal space between rolls so when they are baked, they will cook into each other. Place in oven and bake for 11-15 minutes or until rolls are golden brown. Remove from oven and allow rolls to cool. Reduce temperature of oven to 350 degrees F. In small bowl, combine mustard, poppy seeds and black pepper. Using a long, bread knife, carefully cut rolls in half so they form two, large, bread sheets. Using spatula, coat both sides of bread with mustard. Completely cover bottom bread sheet with ham slices. Completely cover ham slices with Swiss cheese slices. Evenly cover onions over Swiss cheese slices. Carefully place top bread sheet over onions, ham and cheese. Unroll enough aluminum foil to encase sandwich sheet. Spray foil with cooking spray and place sandwich sheet on foil. Seal foil over entire sandwich sheet and place onto cookie sheet. Place back into oven and bake for 25 minutes. Remove from oven and remove foil. Cut into mini sandwiches by using roll indentations as a guide. Arrange sliders on platter and keep warm until ready to serve. Makes 64 sliders.

Buffalo Chicken Tartlets

For Mixture:
2	10 oz. cans chunk chicken, drained and shredded
1/2	cup yellow onion, diced
1	8 oz. package cream cheese, softened
1	3 oz. container crumbled blue cheese
1	cup blue cheese dressing
3/4	cup pepper sauce
1	1/2 cups Cheddar cheese, shredded
1	T hot sauce

For Tartlet:
3	packages (15 count) mini Fillo shells
	Fresh parsley, for garnish

For Mixture: In large frying pan over medium heat, saute onions until caramelized. Add chicken, hot sauce and pepper sauce and cook until ingredients are hot. Remove from heat and pour mixture into large bowl. Stir in cream cheese, blue cheese and blue cheese dressing. Set aside. **For Tartlet:** Preheat oven to 350 degrees F. Place Fillo shells onto cookie sheet. Equally fill Fillo shells with mixture. Place in oven for 20 minutes. Remove from oven and place tartlets on platter. Garnish with parsley. Keep warm until ready to serve. Makes 45 tartlets.

Cheesy Chili Dog Bites

12	large flour tortillas
12	8 inch all beef hot dogs
2	cups Monterey Jack cheese, grated
2	cups Cheddar cheese, grated
1	cup water
2	small cans beef chili
1/2	cup sour cream, for garnish

Preheat oven to 350 degrees F. Mix chili with water and evenly spread on bottom of casserole dish. Set aside. Microwave flour tortillas in plastic wrap for 1 minute until tortillas become soft. Place one hot dog on end of flour tortilla and roll until hot dog is encased in tortilla. Repeat process until all hot dogs are encased in flour tortillas. Place hot dogs on top of chili in casserole dish so each hot dog does not touch. Top encased hot dogs with cheeses. Place in oven uncovered and bake for 20 minutes or until cheese and tortillas start to brown. Take out of oven and cut each hot dog into six equal-sized pieces and discard excess tortillas. Place on serving platter and top with remaining chili from pan and dollop with sour cream. Makes 72 bite-sized appetizers.

Mini Stuffed Dill Potatoes

24	small new potatoes, cut in half
1	large Yukon potato, peeled & diced
1/4	cup minced garlic
1	T rosemary & garlic seasoning
1	T chives
1	t white pepper
1	t black pepper
1/2	cup yellow onion, diced
1	t sea salt
2	sticks butter, melted
1 1/2	cups sour cream
2	T fresh dill, finely chopped

For Topping:

1 1/2	cups Monterey Jack cheese, grated
1 1/2	cups Cheddar cheese, grated
2	T fresh dill, finely chopped
1/2	cup bacon bits (optional)

Preheat oven to 350 degrees F. Cut potatoes and place in large pot. Fill with water and boil on stove top for 25 minutes, until tender. Drain and cool potatoes. Using a small spoon, scoop out small potato halves and place in mixing bowl with cooked, diced potatoes. Using hand mixer, combine potatoes with remaining ingredients. Place potato halves on greased, cookie sheet and evenly distribute mixture into potato halves. **For Topping:** Top each potato half with cheeses, dill and bacon bits (optional). Place in oven and bake for 25 minutes. Remove from heat and place in heated chaffing dish and serve. Makes 48 mini potatoes.

Three-Layer Bean Dip with Blue Corn Tortilla Chips

1	lb. ground beef,cooked & drained
1	8 oz. package cream cheese, softened
1	cup sour cream
1	8 oz. can refried beans
1	8 oz. can kidney beans,drained & mashed
1/2	package (1 oz.) taco seasoning mix
3	t hot sauce
2	T dried parsley
1/2	cup green onions, chopped
1	16 oz. package shredded Cheddar cheese
&	Monterey Jack cheese, grated
2	t white pepper

Preheat oven to 350 degrees F. In medium bowl, blend together ground beef, cream cheese and sour cream. Mix in the refried beans, taco seasoning, hot sauce, parsley, green onions, white pepper and half of the Cheddar/Monterey Jack cheese mixture. Transfer the mixture to an 8 x 12 inch baking dish. Top with remaining Cheddar and Monterey Jack cheeses. Bake in oven 20 to 30 minutes, until cheese is slightly browned. Transfer dip into heated chaffing dish or decorative serving bowl. Serve with Blue Corn tortilla chips. Serves 50.

Chocolate Covered Cake Pops

2	18.5 oz. packages chocolate fudge cake mix
2	small containers chocolate fudge icing
2	t cayenne pepper
2	cups water
6	eggs
1/2	cup oil

50-60	lollipop sticks or wooden corn skewers
2	blocks green floral foam
1	decorative container, vase or bowl of choice

Preheat oven to 350 degree F. Grease two 13 x 9 inch cake pans. In large mixing bowl, using hand mixer, combine cake mix with pepper, eggs and oil. Pour batter evenly between cake pans. Place in oven and bake for 30 minutes or until a toothpick inserted into the center of the cake comes out clean. Remove from oven and cool. In large mixing bowl, crumble cake into a fine texture. Add 1 cup of icing to cake and mix with hands until cake forms a "dough". With damp hands, roll dough into 11/4 inch balls. Place open container of icing into microwave and heat in 15 second intervals until icing is a good dipping consistency. Dip tip of a skewer into icing mixture and insert into cake balls. Repeat process until every cake ball has a skewer. Place cake pops into freezer for 1 hour to firm. Place one block of floral foam onto a sheet of wax paper. Carefully dip skewered, cake balls into icing and rotate skewer until excess icing is removed. Insert skewers into foam and allow to dry until all cake pops are tacky to the touch. Cut the other floral foam to fit inside of desired container for display. Arrange dipped cake pops to form a bouquet. Loosely cover with plastic wrap and refrigerate until two hours before serving. Place on buffet table and enjoy.
Makes 50-60 cake pops.

Chocolate Chocolate Chip Cookies

1	cup shortening
4	T salted butter, softened
1 1/2	cups dark brown sugar
2	eggs
2	t vanilla extract
3	T chocolate syrup
1	t white pepper
1	t nutmeg
2 1/4	cups all-purpose flour
1	t baking soda
1	11.5 oz. package chocolate morsels

Preheat oven to 375 degrees F. In large bowl, using hand mixer, cream together shortening, butter and sugar. Add eggs one at a time, beating well after each addition. Stir in vanilla and chocolate syrup. In separate bowl, combine flour, white pepper, baking soda and nutmeg. Gradually stir dry ingredients into cream mixture and stir in chocolate morsels. Drop mixture by teaspoons in batches onto ungreased, cookie sheets. Bake for 8 to 10 minutes. Remove from oven and place cookies onto wire rack to cool completely and arrange on platter. Makes 5 dozen cookies.

Peach Cobbler Crescents

3	cans crescent rolls (8 count)
2	small cans peaches, drained and cut in half
1/4	cup flour
1/4	cup peach preserves
1	stick butter, melted
1	T cinnamon
1	T pumpkin pie spice
3	T dark brown sugar
1	t ground cloves
1	t vanilla extract

Preheat oven to 350 degrees F. In mixing bowl, dredge peaches with flour and combine with butter, vanilla, preserves, sugar and spices. Unroll crescent rolls and cut each triangle in half. Place onto greased, cookie sheets. Spoon mixture evenly onto center of dough triangles. Roughly pinch edges together and place in oven and bake for 15 to 20 minutes or until golden brown. Remove from oven and cool on baking racks. Arrange on platter and serve.
Makes 48 crescents.

FundaMENU 11

Surf & Turf

Shrimp Toasts with Horseradish Sauce

☾

Creamy Salmon & Rice Pinwheels with Wasabi Sauce

☾

Sausage, Cheese & Mushroom Rolls

☾

Sweet & Sour Meatballs

☾

Cherry Tomato, Basil & Mozzarella Skewers

☾

Ginger Oatmeal Cookies

☾

Banana Pudding Shots

☾

Peanut Butter Bars

Shrimp Toasts with Horseradish Sauce

12	slices white sandwich bread
1	lb. shrimp, peeled & deveined
1/8	cup corn starch
1/4	cup green onions, chopped
1/2	cup sesame seeds
1	avocado, peeled, pitted and diced
1	egg
1	t ground ginger
1	t white pepper
1	t Old Bay seasoning
	corn oil, for frying
1/4	cup sesame oil, for frying

For Horseradish Sauce:

2	cups ketchup
4	T horseradish
1/2	t Old Bay seasoning

Place all ingredients in food processor and pulse until mixture forms a thick paste. Cut crusts off of bread and cut each slice into four equal pieces. Spoon mixture by the teaspoons onto each bread piece, making sure to completely coat entire surface of bread. Place oils into bottom of frying pan and heat on high. Drop shrimp toasts, shrimp side down into oil. Fry until golden brown on each side. Place fried toasts onto paper towel to absorb excess oil. **For Horseradish Sauce:** In small bowl, mix together all ingredients. Place in decorative bowl and serve. Place toasts in heated chaffing dish or serve room temperature with dipping sauce.
Makes 48 toasts.

Creamy Salmon & Rice Pinwheels with Wasabi Sauce

For Rice:
2   cups Sushi rice, rinsed
3   cups water
2   T rice wine vinegar
1   T sugar

For Roll:
6   Nori sheets, (dried, roasted seaweed)
1/2   lb. raw Sushi-grade salmon, flaked
1   8 oz. package cream cheese, softened
1   large carrot, grated
1   seedless cucumber, peeled & cut into thin strips
2   avocados, peeled, pitted & cut into thin slices
1/2   cup capers

For Sauce:
2   cups soy sauce
3   T wasabi paste

For Rice: Place rice, water, sugar and vinegar into saucepan over high heat. Cover and bring to a boil. Reduce heat to low and cook for 15 minutes or until water is absorbed. Remove from heat, stirring every few minutes and cool completely. **For Rolls:** Place Nori sheet (shiny side down) on a sushi mat. Using damp hands, spread rice evenly over Nori, making sure to leave a slight border around edges. Spread a thin layer of cream cheese over rice. Place salmon horizontally across the bottom edge of mat, facing you. Place avocado on top of salmon, followed by capers, carrot and cucumber. Using sushi mat, roll up mixture away from you to seal roll. Repeat process with remaining Nori sheets. Place rolls into plastic wrap and refrigerate until ready to serve. **For Sauce:** In small bowl, using wire whisk, combine soy sauce and wasabi paste. **To Serve:** Take rolls out of plastic wrap and cut each roll into 8 pieces. Place on chilled platter and drizzle with sauce. Serve remaining sauce in small bow with Sushi. Makes 48 pinwheels.

Sausage, Cheese & Mushroom Rolls

2	containers French loaf dough
2	small cans sliced mushrooms, drained
1	lb. ground sausage
1	cup yellow onions, diced
2	cups Cheddar cheese
2	cups Muenster cheese
4	T dried oregano
1	t black pepper
2	T dried basil
1	egg, beaten

Preheat oven to 350 degrees F. Place sausage into large saucepan over medium heat. Add onions, oregano and pepper. Cook until sausage is thoroughly cooked. Remove from heat and drain. Place sausage into large bowl. Add cheeses and mushrooms. Mix until cheese melts slightly. Unroll French loaf onto piece of parchment paper. Spoon half of mixture evenly over dough, allowing a small space around edges. Carefully roll dough into a log. Completely seal edges and pinch the sides of roll to encase mixture. Repeat process with second roll. Place rolls onto a large, greased cookie sheet, allowing plenty of room for the dough to rise. Brush egg wash evenly over rolls. Place in oven and bake for 30-35 minutes or until rolls are golden brown. Remove from heat and allow to cool completely. Cut into 20-25 quarter inch slices and arrange on platter. Serve room temperature. Makes 40-50 spiral appetizers.

Sweet & Sour Meatballs

3	lbs. ground beef
2	cups garlic bread crumbs
3	eggs
1	T white pepper
1	t sea salt
1/2	cup Worcestershire sauce
1	cup scallions, finely diced
2	T dried basil
3	cups sweet & sour sauce

Preheat oven to 375 degrees F. In large mixing bowl, mix together ground beef and scallions. Add eggs, Worcestershire sauce, pepper, salt, basil and bread crumbs. Using hands, shape mixture into 1.5 inch balls and place onto greased cookie sheet. Place in oven and bake for 25-30 minutes or until balls are 155 degrees in the center of each ball. Remove from oven and cool until meatballs harden slightly. Place into crock pot or heated chaffing dish. Microwave sweet and sour sauce for 4 minutes until warm. Carefully pour mixture over meatballs. Garnish with fresh basil. Serve with toothpicks or small, wooden skewers. Serves 50.

Cherry Tomato, Basil & Mozzarella Skewers

2	small containers grape tomatoes (20-30 per package)
2	small containers mini Mozzarella balls (20-30 per package)
1	bunch fresh basil, (leaves only)
1	cup Balsamic vinegar
1	t sea salt
1	t black pepper
50	toothpicks
1/2	cantaloupe, for base

Place tomatoes and Mozzarella into large bowl. Toss with Balsamic vinegar. Pierce one Mozzarella ball with toothpick, leaving one inch from the bottom. Add one basil leaf, followed by one tomato. Insert toothpick into cantaloupe half (flesh side down on platter). Repeat process until all skewers have been made. Sprinkle with salt and pepper and serve at room temperature. Makes 50-60 skewers.

Ginger Oatmeal Cookies

1	cup (2 sticks) salted butter,softened
1	cup firmly packed brown sugar
1/2	cup granulated sugar
3	eggs
1	t vanilla extract
1 1/2	cups all-purpose flour
1	t baking soda
1 1/2	t cinnamon
1	t nutmeg
1	t ground ginger
1	t cloves
1/2	t salt
3	cups Quaker Oats,quick oats
2	cups candied ginger, chopped

Preheat oven to 350 degrees F. In large bowl using hand mixer, beat together butter and sugars until creamy. Add eggs and vanilla extract; beat well. Add flour, baking soda, cinnamon, ginger, nutmeg, cloves and salt. Mix well. Slowly stir in oats and candied ginger. Roll into 1 inch balls and place on cookie sheet. Press down until dough forms a flat circle. Bake 15 minutes or until golden brown. Cool 1 minute on sheet, remove to wire rack. Makes 4 1/2 dozen cookies.

Banana Pudding Shots

4	small packages instant banana pudding mix
8	cups milk
1	box vanilla wafers
1	t vanilla extract
6	bananas, peeled and sliced
2	T butter
2	T brown sugar

For Topping:

10	egg whites
2	T sugar
50	plastic shot glasses

Preheat oven to 350 degrees F. In large mixing bowl, using hand mixer, combine milk with vanilla extract and pudding mix. Blend until smooth and refrigerate for 15 minutes. In large, greased casserole dish, layer half box of vanilla wafers. Spread half of pudding mixture over wafers. Repeat process. **For Topping**: In small mixing bowl, using hand mixer, beat egg whites. Gradually add sugar and beat until soft peaks form. Evenly spread mixture over pudding. Place in oven and bake for 10-15 minutes or until egg whites turn golden brown. Remove from oven and allow to cool. In saucepan over medium heat melt butter and brown sugar. Add banana slices and cook until both sides of banana are golden brown. Arrange shot glasses on platters and evenly distribute pudding into shot glasses. Garnish with banana slice and serve with small, wooden serving spoons. Serves 50.

Peanut Butter Bars

For Crust:
1/2   cup margarine, melted
1.5   cups Graham cracker crumbs
1/4   cup sugar

For Filling:
2   8 oz. packages cream cheese, softened
1/2   tub whipped topping
1.5   cups creamy peanut butter
1/2   lb. confectioners sugar
1   t vanilla extract

Preheat oven to 350 degrees F. **For Crust:** In mixing bowl, stir together ingredients until combined. Grease 1 large cookie sheet (with 1 inch edge) and press mixture firmly on bottom of pan. Bake for 10-15 minutes until golden. Remove from oven and cool. **For Filling:** In large bowl, using hand mixer, cream together peanut butter, cream cheese and sugar. Add vanilla extract. Refrigerate for two hours. Remove from refrigerator and spread mixture evenly over crust. Top with whipped topping. Cut into 50-60 bite-sized squares. Arrange on platter and serve. Makes 50-60 servings.

FundaMENUS

Chapter 12
Cost-Effective Cocktails

 lcohol is always the biggest expense when hosting a dinner party for a large number of guests. Although it is proper etiquette for guests to bring a bottle of wine or liquor when invited to a special dinner gathering, it is also the host's responsibility to make sure that the cocktails are constantly flowing throughout the evening. With that sentiment in mind, I concocted seven, very cost-effective cocktails that have no problems in the flavor department and are even more special because they are designed to go easy on the bank account.

Each specialty cocktail can be made for under $20 and yield at least one gallon of libation... And that is before adding the ice! The secret is purchasing cheaper bottles of alcohol for mixing cocktails in large quantities. For instance, the Red Wine Sangria recipe described within this chapter, uses Bay Bridge wines, which are usually on sale at my local grocery store for less than three dollars per bottle. Because the alcohol is being mixed with other ingredients, the difference in flavor compared to a more expensive brand of alcohol is very minimal. And that is a savings that can keep any dinner party under budget.

Cost-Effective Cocktails

Blueberry Martini

☾

Peach Tea Martini

☾

Red Wine Sangria

☾

Pineapple & Rum Spritzer

☾

Tomato, Cucumber & Dill Martini

☾

Gin & Grapefruit Tonic

☾

Pink Lemon Lime Punch

Blueberry Martini

2   quarts blueberry juice
1   750 ml bottle vodka
1   cup lime juice
1   small container fresh blueberries, for garnish

In large, one gallon pitcher or jug, mix blueberry juice, vodka and lime juice. Cover container and refrigerate until ready to serve.
To Serve: Pour mixture into a martini shaker with ice and 10 blueberries. Shake vigorously for 30 seconds. Pour into large martini glasses. Garnish with blueberries. **Note:** A Martini shaker makes two large cocktails. Repeat process to make more cocktails. Makes 12 large or 24 small Martinis.

Peach Tea Martini

1	packet low calorie peach tea mix
2	quarts water
1	12 oz. can peach nectar
1	750 ml bottle sweet tea vodka
2	large peaches, pitted & sliced, for garnish

In large, one gallon pitcher or jug, mix peach tea mix with water. Add vodka and peach nectar. Cover container and refrigerate until ready to serve. **To Serve**: Pour mixture into a Martini shaker with ice. Shake vigorously for 30 seconds. Pour into large Martini glasses. Garnish with peach slices. **Note:** A Martini shaker makes two large cocktails. Repeat process to make more cocktails. Makes 12 or more cocktails.

Red Wine Sangria

4	750 ml bottles cheap red wine
2	12 ounce cans sprite
2	navel oranges, sliced
2	lemons, sliced
2	limes, sliced
2	grapefruit, sliced
2	kiwis, sliced
2	cups pineapple juice

In large, two gallon punch bowl or pitcher, mix wine with fruit and pineapple juice. Cover and refrigerate overnight or until ready to serve. **To Serve:** Fill tumbler glasses halfway full of ice. Pour 1/3 cup sprite over ice in each tumbler glass. Pour Sangria over sprite and ice. Stir. Garnish with sliced fruit from sangria mixture. Makes 12 large or 24 small cocktails.

Pineapple & Rum Spritzer

2	quarts pineapple juice
1	750 ml bottle rum
2	cups Triple Sec
2	liters ginger ale
2	oranges, thinly sliced, for garnish

In large, two gallon punch bowl or pitcher, mix pineapple juice with rum and Triple Sec. Cover and refrigerate overnight or until ready to serve. **To Serve:** Add ginger ale to mixture and stir. Fill tall tumbler glasses halfway with ice. Pour cocktail over ice in each tumbler glass. Garnish cocktail with orange slices. Makes 12 or more cocktails.

Tomato, Cucumber & Dill Martini

2   quarts Mrs. T's Spicy Bloody Mary Mix
1   seedless cucumber, thinly sliced
1   750 ml bottle vodka
3   stalks fresh dill, plus some for garnish
1   seedless cucumber, thinly sliced, for garnish

In large, one gallon pitcher or jug, mix bloody Mary mix with vodka. Add cucumber and dill. Cover container and refrigerate for at least two days before serving. **To Serve:** Pour mixture into a Martini shaker with ice. Shake vigorously for 30 seconds. Pour into large Martini glasses. Garnish with cucumber and fresh dill. **Note:** A Martini shaker makes two large cocktails. Repeat process to make more cocktails. Makes 12 or more cocktails.

Gin & Grapefruit Tonic

2	quarts ruby red grapefruit juice
2	12 oz. cans La Croix Grapefruit Sparkling Water
1	liter bottle tonic water
1	cup lime juice
1	750 ml bottle gin
2	grapefruit, thinly sliced & cut into thirds

In large, one gallon punch bowl or pitcher, mix grapefruit juice with gin and lime juice. Cover and refrigerate overnight or until ready to serve. **To Serve:** Just before serving, add tonic and sparkling water to mixture. Fill tumbler glasses halfway with ice. Pour cocktail over ice in each tumbler glass. Garnish cocktail with grapefruit slices. Makes 12 or more cocktails.

Pink Lemon Lime Punch

1   packet low calorie pink lemonade mix
2   quarts water
1   cup lemon juice
1   cup lime juice
2   liters lemon lime soda
1   750 ml bottle citron vodka
2   lemons, thinly sliced, for garnish

In large, two gallon punch bowl or pitcher, mix pink lemonade mix with water. Add lemon and lime juice and vodka. Cover and refrigerate overnight or until ready to serve. **To Serve:** Just before serving, add lemon lime soda into mixture. Fill tall tumbler glasses halfway with ice. Pour cocktail over ice in each tumbler glass. Garnish cocktail with lemon slices. Makes 12 or more cocktails.

*Funda*MENUS

Chapter 13
Points of Presentation

t's a well-known fact that hosting a successful dinner party requires great-tasting food. However, presenting great-tasting food in a manner that enhances the flavor experience for dinner guests is sometimes much harder to achieve than actually preparing the food... Especially on a budget. Most novice party hosts fall short on what well-presented food means.

The decorating budget does not have to focus solely on buying expensive flowers and setting them in a center of a table with over-priced fine China. Presentation simply does not have to break the bank and the following tips will give the novice host a new perspective on how to achieve a stunning presentation without going over budget.

Tablecloths, Placemats & Table Runners

Setting a stunning dinner table for eight to 12 guests is very simple if you start from the bottom of the table and work your way up from there. So, with that in mind, all great table settings start with a tablecloth. Tablecloths can be made out of practically anything. I have used traditional tablecloths, but I prefer to use whatever I have lying around the inside of my house, outside in my yard or have sitting on a shelf in my storage shed. I have used metal flashing, bed sheets, fall leaves, leftover roofing, curtains, wrapping paper, bolts of fabric and remnants of canvas from artwork for tablecloths. However, if you have your heart set on a traditional tablecloth, try purchasing one from a local yard sale or thrift store. Most thrift stores have a wide variety of shapes and sizes and usually they can be purchased for under $10. Another alternative to a tablecloth are placemats or table runners. I have a few different patterns of placemats that I purchased at various yard sales and I recently bought twelve matching linen placemats at my local dollar store for a very affordable $12, plus tax!

Centerpieces & Flowers

A fabulous dinner party needs to have a stunning centerpiece. That doesn't mean that a boat-load of money needs to be spent on flowers. Some of my most beautiful centerpieces were created by utilizing objects found inside my home or cutting greenery and flowers from my back yard. Since I live in the south, I have a huge Hydrangea bush that yields hundreds of bulbous flowers that bloom in May through July. I cut and dry the remaining Hydrangea flowers so I can use them in arrangements throughout the year for any occasion. I use greenery from my Holly and Gardenia bushes to add interest and color to my floral designs. Outdoor small, potted plants and moss found outside in the back yard can also be used for a gorgeous centerpiece. Just make sure that the outside of the pots are clean and free from wear and tear.

Some of my favorite centerpieces that I have created didn't use flowers at all. For one tablescape that I designed recently, I purchased 100 peacock feathers on **Ebay** for $40 and placed them into three, slender, varying-sized, cylindrical vases. I then filled 20, miscellaneous-sized glasses with blue-tinted water and floated a tea candle in each glass and placed them horizontally across the entire length of my dining room table. The effect was quite stunning and I only spent money on the peacock feathers and tea candles.

Another great idea for centerpieces is incorporating Christmas decorations into your tablescape. Ball ornaments, such as clear glass or silver can make an impact on any table. Non-Christmas-themed decorations such as ornate, wire ribbon or crystallized branches can be incorporated with other home-found objects to create an amazing table design. For one of my more recent dinner party tables, I used an assortment of cylindrical vases and filled them with varying sizes of disco balls that I purchased at a craft store. I flipped each of the filled vases onto round mirrors and decorated the remainder of the table with tea candles and more disco balls. The effect was very modern and sophisticated, and none of my guests ever noticed the absence of flowers.

Dinnerware, Glasses & Napkins

Most people think that throwing an upscale dinner party requires the food to be presented on fine China and gilded chargers, with cloth napkins, beautiful flatware and a gorgeous center piece. Well, like most people, I agree. But, that doesn't mean that one needs to go out and spend a fortune on these items - just be smart and creative about the table theme. And remember, a good table setting doesn't need to match, it just needs to appear to be cohesive.

For me, shopping for China at thrift stores is the best way to go when it comes to impressing the dinner guests when you are on a tight budget. For instance, I had wanted a matching China set for ages that would accommodate 12 people. I looked online and found that purchasing a used China set on **Ebay** was out of my price range because of the high shipping costs. I gave myself a $100 budget for my China purchase and headed to a few of my favorite, local, thrift stores. I immediately found a great set of 12, matching gold-rimmed plates and 12, similar-patterned tea cups from a different set. I purchased everything for eight dollars! Excited by my discovery, I went to a few more thrift stores and, as luck would have it, I kept finding items from the same two China sets.

The next month, I found a matching set of vintage Noritake China that was in excellent condition that had 65 pieces, including two, large platters, a gravy boat and three, various-sized serving bowls. I purchased that set for $49! After researching my purchase on the internet, I found out that the whole set turned out to be worth over $800! Now I have three different sets of China that I can mix and match to accommodate up to 24 guests and I only paid a grand total of $89!

A similar situation happened when I purchased my cloth dinner napkins. I found two sets of 12 napkins (one set is green, and the other is white) that I bought from two thrift stores, totaling only $10. My wine glasses (from two sets) were purchased at a garage sale for $12 and I purchased 24 gold chargers from **Amazon.com** for $49. My flatware for 24 guests was purchased from **Ikea** for $40. The total price for an entire table setting to accommodate 24 guests, including serving platters, came to a "grand" total of $200!

Setting the Table

Now that the tableware is taken care of, it's time to talk about din-nerware table setting placement. I usually anchor my dinnerware with chargers. Chargers are a very affordable way to dress up any table design. There are a wide variety of designs that are on sale on **Amazon.com** and there always seems to be a closeout design for sale at a very affordable price.

The dinner plate is placed onto the center of each charger. I then place the salad plate on top of the dinner plate. (**Note:** If you are planning on serving an appetizer course before the salad, keep the appetizer plates on a prep table for time-efficient plating until you are ready to serve the appetizer.) A soup bowl is placed on top of the salad plate. I usually finish my dinnerware design with a folded cloth napkin. My favorite napkin fold is a classic one. It is called a **"Bishop's Miter"**. I prefer placing each folded napkin into the empty soup bowl. Easy, step by step instructional videos on how to create the **"Bishop's Miter"** napkin fold can be found on **Youtube.com**.

Forks are placed to the left of each dinner plate. The largest fork is always placed closest to the plate and the smaller fork is placed far-thest from the plate. I always set my tables with two forks, although, if you can only afford to have one fork at the dinner table, it is perfectly acceptable among friends. The table knife (or steak knife, depending on the menu) is placed on the right hand side of the dinner plate and a soup spoon is placed beside the knife/knives, the farthest right from the dinner plate. A water goblet is placed slightly right at the top of the dinner plate and a wine glass or cock-

Setting the Table

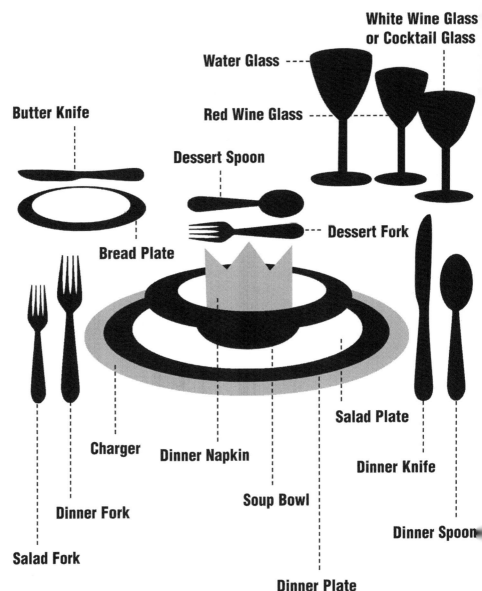

White Wine Glass or Cocktail Glass

Water Glass

Butter Knife

Red Wine Glass

Dessert Spoon

Dessert Fork

Bread Plate

Salad Plate

Charger   Dinner Napkin

Dinner Knife

Dinner Fork

Soup Bowl

Dinner Spoon

Salad Fork

Dinner Plate

tail glass is placed directly above the knives and spoons. Dessert forks and spoons are placed horizontally above the dinner plate.

Food Service for Four-Course Dinner Parties

Once all of the dinner guests have sat down at the dinner table and have placed their napkins onto their laps, gather all of the salad plates and soup bowls from the table and place them onto a prep table or kitchen counter. Allow the guests to pour the wine while you are preparing the salad course. Toss the salad and evenly distribute the salad onto the salad plates. Place the salad plates back onto the table and sit down with your guests and enjoy the first course.

When all the guests have eaten their salad, remove the plates and quickly place them into the sink. Ladle the soup into soup bowls from a heated crock pot or sauce pan from the stove top and serve. Quickly prep any "loose ends" for the main course, then sit back down with the guests to enjoy the soup course. Collect the bowls at the end of the course and place them into the sink with the other dishes.

Retrieve the dinner plates from the dining room table and prepare the main course. (**Note:** Take this time to encourage the guests to get up from the dinner table to mingle, replenish cocktails or use the lavatory while the main course is being finalized. This way, the flow of the dinner party does not feel like an awkward transition for the main course). Plate and serve the main course when all the guests have returned to their seats. Enjoy the main course with your guests. After having an enjoyable conversation at the dinner table over a wonderful main course, collect the plates and place them into the sink for cleaning.

Plating desserts for a dinner party mainly depends on which dessert you plan to serve that evening. Most cakes, cheesecakes, and pies can be cut ahead of time and plated onto dessert plates or bowls and held at room temperature until they are ready to serve. Cutting and plating desserts in front of the guests is an added bonus, but it is wise to only do so if you are completely comfortable with your plating skills. Coffee or tea, as well as dessert wines and cordials can be brought to the table at this time, if guests want these items with their desserts. Remember to stay calm and relaxed throughout the entire dinner party. A good host does not look like they are anxious or nervous.

Buffet Table Presentation

The best buffet table set-ups are ones that look as good as they taste. So many buffet parties that I have attended fall short on presentation. The biggest mistake for setting up a dinner buffet is serving all the food items flatly onto a bare, dinner table. All great buffet presentations have one thing in common and that is what I call, **"Step-Ability"**. A buffet table should incorporate varying steps of height, to make the food just as visually-pleasing as the food tastes.

To achieve a stunning **"Step-Ability"** on a buffet, start by placing various-shaped card board boxes, plastic bins or large pans (flipped over) onto a naked table. Make sure to place a box in the center of the table for the centerpiece. Place fabric of your liking completely over the boxes. (**Note:** Make sure that the boxes are sturdy enough to hold a good amount of weight. For fire-safety reasons, it is best to place any chaffing dishes directly onto the fabric-decorated table.) Drape a second layer of fabric over sections of the buffet. Place the plated food onto the different heights of the fabric-laden boxes. A multi-tiered food tower is also a good purchase to show-case desserts or small appetizers. Place flowers, decorations or can-dles into the small spaces created by the boxes. Handwrite or print out name cards of each recipe featured on the buffet table. Make sure to include basic food allergy information such as using walnuts in a recipe. Place the centerpiece onto the middle back box and the entire buffet is ready for consumption. The rest of the evening is free for you to spend quality time with your special guests!

Enjoy the Party!

For Recipe Photography
& Entertaining Tips. Log onto...

*Funda*MENUS.COM

FundaMENUS

Chapter 14

Recipe Index

A

B

e

F

G

H

L

$\mathcal{T}$

$\mathcal{V}$

$\mathcal{W}$

For Recipe Photography
& Entertaining Tips, Log onto...

*Funda*MENUS.COM

24555496R00081

Made in the USA
Charleston, SC
30 November 2013